On My Way to School

by Mark Weakland   illustrated by Rea Zhai

PICTURE WINDOW BOOKS
a capstone imprint

Jayla

Name: **Jayla**

Birthday: **August 13**

Favorite color: **orange**

Favorite food: **tacos**

Favorite animal: **giraffe**

I want to be a: **pro soccer player**

Table of Contents

On Our Way to School

Good morning! My name is Jayla, and I'm on my way to school. Now that you are here, you can come with me! Every morning millions of kids go to school. Every afternoon they go back home. Students around the world travel to school in so many ways. Let's take a look and see how they do it.

Big Yellow Bus

Lots of kids go to school in a big yellow bus. The trip starts when the bus doors open. Climb the steps and find your seat! A large bus like this one carries dozens of students. When everyone is safely sitting, the doors close, and the bus rumbles down the road. The bus may go straight to school or stop a few times along the way.

YOUR TURN! What do you think it sounds like on a school bus? What do you hear on your way to school?

Getting a Lift

Not all school buses are big. Some are about half the size of a full-sized bus. School vans are even smaller. When just a few kids ride together, they get to know each other pretty well.

Smaller buses and vans may have a lift. It gives students who can't stand or walk a little boost. That's my friend Miles in the orange shirt. The lift moves his wheelchair into the bus.

Go Far in a Car

Buses aren't the only way to get to school.
Lots of students ride in a car. Traveling in
a car is easy. Jump in a booster seat, click
your seatbelt, and off you go! Some families
carpool. They work together so the adults
in each family take turns driving. One week
Ollie's mom drives. The next week it's Emma's
grandpa. This week Mr. Hernandez is driving
the kids to school.

NO PARKING
8 AM – 10 AM

2 HOUR
PARKING

Step by Step

Long ago, before cars and buses, most students walked to school. Today, some still do. They think it's great to be outside. I agree! You feel the wind on your face and hear birds singing. To keep walkers safe, crossing guards stop traffic while kids cross the street. In some neighborhoods, students join a "walking school bus." They walk in a long line with a few adults.

YOUR TURN! What do you think these kids see on their walk to school? What do you see on your way to school?

Rolling Down the Tracks

In some big cities, students rumble down tracks instead of roads. They ride a train or subway to school. Each student carries a fare card. A fare card is like a ticket. It gets you through the gate. Knowing your stops is important. Kids often ride with a group of friends so they know when to get on and off the train. Next stop—school!

YOUR TURN! What do you think it's like to ride a subway to school? How would it be different from riding a bus or walking?

Over Water and Ice

What if water lies between your home and school? You might ride across it on a boat. A ferry is a special boat that regularly carries people across a body of water. Some ferries carry cars, trucks, and buses too. In very cold places, students may need to cross frozen rivers or lakes to get to school. They may ride snowmobiles. I think that would be fun—but *brrr!*

YOUR TURN! Think about all the ways kids go to school. What's your favorite? Why would you want to travel to school this way?

Different Places, Different Ways

Not all kids ride to school in a vehicle with an engine. In some parts of the world, students travel by horse and cart. Many others ride bikes. In India you might see kids going to school in a rickshaw. A rickshaw is like a bike and a wagon put together. Climb aboard, squeeze in tight, and hold on!

19

Off to Class!

There are so many ways to travel to school. Roll in a bus or zip in a car. Float in a boat. Ride your bike or take a walk. You can even sit in a cart and be pulled by a horse. No matter how you go, you'll always end up in the same, awesome place—your school!

Glossary

carpool—to travel to a place with others in a single vehicle; carpool members usually keep a schedule and take turns driving

crossing guard—a person who helps students safely cross a street

dozen—another word for 12

fare—the cost of riding a subway, bus, or other vehicle

ferry—a boat that regularly carries people across a body of water

lift—a machine used to raise and lower people and objects

rickshaw—a three-wheeled vehicle with a driver up front and seats for riders in back

snowmobile—a vehicle with an engine and skis or runners that is used to travel over snow

stop—a place where people get on and off a train, bus, or other vehicle

vehicle—a machine that carries people and goods

Read More

Lyons, Shelly. *Transportation in My Neighborhood.* My Neighborhood. North Mankato, Minn.: Capstone Press, 2013.

O'Connell, Eleanor. *Schools Around the World.* Adventures in Culture. New York: Gareth Stevens Publishing, 2017.

Smith, Penny. *A School Like Mine: A Celebration of Schools Around the World.* Children Just Like Me. New York: DK Publishing, 2016.

Internet Sites

Use FactHound to find Internet sites related to this book.

Visit *www.facthound.com*

Just type in 9781515838487 and go.

Critical Thinking Questions

1. Using this book, make a list of ways in which students can travel to and from school.

2. Turn to pages 8 and 9 and explain what is happening in the illustration.

3. How might you cross a body of water to get to school?

Index

Look for all the books in the series:

Special thanks to our adviser, Sara Hjelmeland, M.Ed., Kindergarten Teacher, for her expertise.

Editor: Jill Kalz
Designer: Lori Bye
Production Specialist: Laura Manthe
The illustrations in this book were created digitally.

Picture Window Books are published by Capstone
1710 Roe Crest Drive, North Mankato, Minnesota 56003
www.mycapstone.com

Library of Congress Cataloging-in-Publication Data is available on the Library of Congress website.
ISBN 978-1-5158-3848-7 (library binding)
ISBN 978-1-5158-4063-3 (paperback)
ISBN 978-1-5158-3854-8 (eBook PDF)
Summary: How do I get to school? While lots of students hop on a bus, *On My Way to School* explores some alternative methods used by kids around the world, including subways, bikes, and boats. It's a transportation treat for young readers, narrated in 1st-person by a fellow student and accompanied by bright, full-color illustrations that embrace diversity.

Shutterstock: jannoon028, (notebook) design element throughout

Printed in China.
966